What's Down There?

By Marla Tomlinson

T0062071

Discover Plants and Animals
Vowel Teams Review

Scan this code to access the Teacher's Notes for this series or visit
www.norwoodhousepress.com/decodables

NORWOOD HOUSE PRESS

DEAR CAREGIVER, *The Decodables* series contains books following a systematic, cumulative phonics scope and sequence aligned with the science of reading. Each book allows its reader to apply their phonics knowledge in engaging and relatable texts. The words within each text have been carefully selected to ensure that readers can rely on their decoding skills as they encounter new or unfamiliar words. They also include high frequency words appropriate for the target skill level of the reader.

When reading these books with your child, encourage them to sound out words that are unfamiliar by attending to the target letter(s) and sounds. If the unknown word is an irregularly spelled high frequency word or a word containing a pattern that has yet to be taught (challenge words) you may encourage your child to attend to the known parts of the word and provide the pronunciation of the unknown part(s). Rereading the texts multiple times will allow your child the opportunity to build their reading fluency, a skill necessary for proficient comprehension.

You can be confident you are providing your child with opportunities to build their decoding abilities which will encourage their independence as they become lifelong readers.

Happy Reading!

Emily Nudds, M.S. Ed Literacy
Literacy Consultant

Norwood House Press • www.norwoodhousepress.com
The Decodables ©2024 by Norwood House Press. All Rights Reserved.
Printed in the United States of America.
367N–082023

Library of Congress Cataloging-in-Publication Data has been filed and is available at https://lccn.loc.gov/2023012392

Literacy Consultant: Emily Nudds, M.S.Ed Literacy
Editorial and Production Development and Management: Focus Strategic Communications Inc.
Editors: Christine Gaba, Christi Davis-Martell
Photo Credits: Shutterstock: Albert Beukhof (p. 19), Andrei Metelev (p. 6), Daniil_98_03_09 (p. 15), DReynoso (p. 18), Fiona M. Donnelly (p. 16), Formatoriginal (p. 20), Galih al gifar (p. 8), JMx Images (p. 21), kost25 (p. 4), Macrovector (covers), Miroslav Hlavko (cover, p. 11), Nannycz (p. 10), Nikolay132 (p. 7), Owsigor (p. 14), P. Qvist (p. 12), Rob Jansen (p. 17), Sebastien Coell (p. 9), Videocorpus (p. 5), Zoltan Tarlacz (p. 13).

Hardcover ISBN: 978-1-68450-684-2   Paperback ISBN: 978-1-68404-906-6
eBook ISBN: 978-1-68404-961-5

Contents

The Ants Are Marching

Your bare feet are on the cool ground. You feel something sneak onto your toe. It is an ant. Why is it there? Where did it come from? It may have come from under your feet! Most ants live deep underground.

FUN FACT

Most ant colonies go about 7 to 10 feet deep.

The longest ant colony in the world is 3,700 miles and goes through Italy, France, and Spain.

Some ants are busy scurrying along a tree.

A cricket is tucked away in his earthy home.

Many bugs and animals make their home under the **soil**. They may do this to stay safe. Or they may get their food there. Some like to stay cool and be out of the heat. They need the right space to call home.

The underground boasts a lot of life!

The Worm Way

Worms may seem gross. They look like they ooze and leak slime. But this all helps them in their **habitat**! Earthworms leak out a type of slime. This slime has stuff in it that is good for soil. It helps the plants grow.

The worm keeps wet in the soil.

Slime also helps the worm. Worms need to keep **damp** to stay alive. The slime is key to staying damp. If a worm's skin dries out, they will die so they need to stay out of a sun ray! The worm has smooth skin that helps them move. The slime may leave a trail as they go.

Worms eat dirt as they dig. They make meals of dead leaves and plants.

Many bugs live underground. They need the damp soil and the food found in the dirt.

Some bugs lay their eggs in the dirt. They hatch as a baby, or larva. Grubs stay underground until they grow. Soon they become adult beetles.

Cicadas also lay their eggs in the ground. These loud bugs may wait many years before coming out.

This cicada has come out of its underground nest.

Bee Below Ground

Have you seen a bumblebee sleep? They can be seen having a snooze on a flower or in some grass. Bumblebees often make their nests in holes left by moles or other small animals. These bees zoom around sweet flower blooms in the heat of the day. Then they head to their home at night, when it is cool.

A bumblebee takes a nap on this flower.

This yellowjacket leaves its nest in the ground.

This home might be in a hole made by mice or other small animals. Bumblebees do not dig their own holes. They look for places that are empty. If there is no hole, they will find a hollow tree or empty birdhouse to call home.

Other bees and wasps will nest in the ground, too, like yellowjackets and mason bees.

Dig a Home

If you find a heap of dirt in the grass that wasn't there before, a mole may have gone by! Moles dig tunnels in the ground as they look for food or make a home. They push the dirt up, making molehills.

They feed on bugs and worms. A mole will stow some bugs to eat later in a room they have made in the dirt.

Moles have front paws that act like a spoon or shovel. This is a tool that helps them scoop the dirt. Each toe has a large nail to help dig.

FUN FACT

Moles can dig 18 feet in an hour!

The mole digs its way out of the ground.

Moles show how well animals **adapt** to their habitat.

Moles do not see well because they stay underground year after year. They stay there almost their whole lives. If they need to find a new place to dig, they might come out.

Their eyes also have fur and extra skin to keep them free of dirt.

Moles have a coat that is smooth. This helps them move in the dirt.

You may find molehills in the grass.

Around Town

Many animals dig a home. Some of these homes are called **burrows**.

Prairie dogs burrow in the ground. Their burrow can have so many homes in it that it is called a town. Between 15 to 26 prairie dog families may live in a town so they are not shy.

Prairie dogs get into their home through a hole that has raised sides. They make these raised sides to protect their home from floods.

Prairie dogs make their home beneath the ground but scoot around on land to feed on grass and leaves.

You may think prairie dogs look more like squirrels than dogs.

A groundhog is a sight you may see in a field. They live in burrows in Canada and the United States. Their burrow can be between 8 and 66 feet long, and it has many rooms and exits.

Groundhogs are true hibernators. This means they go into a deep sleep in winter. They sleep and dream for about three months. It is still cool when they wake up.

This groundhog pokes out of its burrow to see what is going on outside.

This groundhog is out in the sun's rays before going back in his burrow.

A groundhog may greet you as it lies in the sun on a rock. They spend most of their day underground. But in the summer they take naps in the warm midday sun. They like the heat.

FUN FACT

Groundhogs are also called whistle pigs because they make a high squeal sound. They are called woodchucks, too, even though they do not "chuck" wood!

15

Chipmunks also live in underground homes. These tiny animals are about the same size as a bar of soap.

They look cute and like to play and run, but they may make tunnels all over! Their home can be three feet deep and go up to 30 feet long.

They eat nuts and seeds. Chipmunks will bring a load of seeds back to their burrow to store for when there is snow.

You may see a chipmunk peeking out of its burrow or around a rock or log.

This armadillo is out for a night walk.

In some hot places you might see an **odd** animal that may give you a fright! An armadillo has hair and scales. They have a long tail and big ears.

These beasts are only about 12 pounds and two to three feet long. They come out at night to find a treat. They eat worms, bugs, and their larva. They may also eat roots and leaves.

Armadillos sleep in a burrow. They spend 16 hours a day asleep. Then they stray at night to try to find food.

An armadillo does not sleep with other armadillos. But they might share their home with snakes or rats.

Snakes also spend time beneath the ground. Many snakes sleep under trees or in caves.

The gopher snake lives in burrows in the ground. They like **drained** soil that is damp but not too wet.

The gopher snake likes to live in burrows that used to be a gopher house.

Life Beneath the Earth

You see them fly. They weave through the forest. They **soar** high in the sky. But some birds go underground, too.

The burrowing owl makes a nest in a burrow. They can make their own home but often take burrows for their homes. These owls hunt at night and see well in the dark. They live in grasslands. They do not live in forests like many other owls.

The kingfisher is a bird who also makes a nest in the ground. They use their beak to dig into the **banks** of rivers or streams to make their home. This is a good spot for these blue and red birds. They feast on fish.

This burrowing owl is protecting its home.

Rabbits are good at digging. Their claws are digging tools. They dig connecting tunnels called a warren. Up to 30 rabbits may live in one large warren. The warren has many ways to get in or out. A rabbit can zoom into an opening when it is chased.

A rabbit might have its burrow near you!

To get their meal, a kingfisher will swoop into the water and grab a fish.

As you can see, there is a lot of life underground.

From the worm to the mole, underground homes give a safe place to live. They also make it easy for the animals to find food and water.

Next time you are outside, think about what might be making its home underground!

Glossary

adapt: change to survive

banks: edges of waterways

burrows (bər-ōz): animal homes dug underground

damp: wet, moist

drained: had water go through to make wet

habitat: the natural place where an animal or plant lives

odd: weird, strange

soar (sōr): go high in the sky

soil: land/dirt with nutrients in it

Index

Vowel Teams

ea/ee/ey			oa/oe/ow	ai/ay		ie/igh
beak	heat	seen	below	day	stray	die
beasts	key	sleep	boasts	drained	tail	fright
bee	leak	sneak	burrow	lay	trail	high
deep	leave	squeal	coat	may	wait	might
dream	meal	streams	grow	nail	way	night
feast	near	sweet	hollow	play		right
feed	need	three	load	raised		sight
feel	see	weave	snow	ray		
feet	seeds	year	soap	stay		
greet	seem		stow			
heap			toe			

oo/ue			y as vowel		Vowel team two syllable word
blooms	roots	spoon	baby	shy	beneath
blue	scoop	swoop	by	sky	prairie
cool	scoot	tool	fly	try	staying
food	smooth	true	many	why	
ooze	snooze	zoom			
room	soon				

High-Frequency Words

also	earthy	live	only	through
around	even	most	over	underground
because	give	move	show	world
does	large	new	small	

Challenging Words

armadillo	cicada	hibernators	squirrels	wasps
birdhouse	earthworms	larva	warren	